Introduction to
Card
Making

igloobooks

Published in 2015
by Igloo Books Ltd
Cottage Farm
Sywell
NN6 0BJ
www.igloobooks.com

Cover images © Thinkstock / Getty Images

LEO002 0715
2 4 6 8 10 9 7 5 3 1
ISBN 978-1-78440-281-5

Printed and manufactured in China

Introduction to
Card Making

Contents

Introduction

Cards are the perfect way to express a wide variety of sentiments. Happy Birthday, Congratulations, Get Well Soon, every occasion can be marked with a beautiful card. Cards made by hand add a deeper level of charm, taking the time to carefully construct something lovely and personal is appreciated by both the maker and the receiver.

Putting thought and planning into constructing a card and making it special is exceptionally satisfying. Inside this book, you will find everything that you need to know to get started on what can be an incredibly rewarding hobby.

Make stunning and stylish cards for men, women and children. Say congratulations, thank you and get well soon. For birthdays, easter, weddings, valentine's, christenings, new babies and general every day cards. This book will guide you through the materials and equipment that you need to make your own fantastic cards.

With step-by-step instructions on crafting pretty cards, we will take you through the process of getting started and inspire you to create your very own designs.

Instructions

Whether you've just started making cards or you're already a seasoned crafter, it's often worth taking a look at your card-making essentials to make sure you've got everything you're likely to need.

When you first start out card-making, it's a little like being let loose in a sweet shop. There will be the tendency to do a trolley dash in every hobby shop and craft fair. Many people tend to regret a lot of their early buys, as their experience grows and they develop their own style and preferences. However, many agree on the card-making basics, so this book highlights these along with some other card-making essentials.

Card-making basics:

Adhesives: there's a mind-boggling array of adhesives on the market, but to start with your best bets are: double-sided tape, which can easily be trimmed to size; 3D foam tape or pads to add dimension; and a roller glue that is easy to dispense without making your fingers sticky.

Card: you can never have too much card! To give you flexibility in your designs, try making your own cards, as you can use just about any type and colour imaginable. A stash of white or cream card and envelopes are essential.

Cardstock: available in every shade imaginable and in different weights (thicknesses) to suit, card is essential for matting, making your own cards, creating your own embellishments and much more.

Craft knife: there are many types of craft knives available and they prove indispensable when it comes to cutting and scoring. Invest in one that has a changeable blade, or choose a scalpel.

Cutting mat: you'll need two different types of cutting surface: a self-healing mat for cutting, piercing and setting eyelets, and a PTFE-coated craft mat, preferably infused with glass for strength, non-stick and able to withstand high temperatures.

Decorative papers: there's much to be borrowed from scrapbooking, especially patterned paper, as so many are excellent for card backgrounds and offer good value for money coming in 12x12 in size.

Greetings: items such as rub-ons and peel-off greetings can be much maligned, but do serve a purpose, especially when you're stuck for a greeting in a hurry.

Heat gun: if you're going to be stamping and embossing, then this is an absolute essential. There are several designs to choose from, but it's a good idea to listen to other crafters' advice before you commit to a particular model.

Paper trimmer: essential for cutting pieces for layering and can help you to save money by cutting your own cards, as well as giving you the flexibility to make blanks from any sort of card to co-ordinate with your designs.

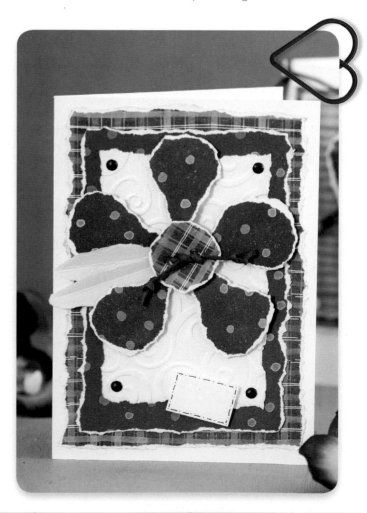

Scoring board and bone folder: a bone folder to give you a nice finish to the card folds and a scoring board to get the proportions correct.

Scissors: a large pair of kitchen scissors is fine for non-precision cutting, whereas you're likely to need a very small precision-tip pair for all the fiddly jobs that require pinpoint accuracy. You'll also be thankful for a pair of small Teflon-coated scissors to cut sticky materials with minimum hassle.

Things you might need:

Chalk inks: chalk inks are wonderful for creating backgrounds, just by sweeping across plain card. If you're not sure what you need, a number of inks are available in small sizes and can be the ideal low-cost choice for experimentation.

Craft knife and metal ruler: for cutting precision, particularly on shorter pieces and fiddly bits, this is essential. You should also avoid using wooden rulers.

Dies: metal dies are incredibly useful for cutting paper, card and other materials into specific shapes.
They come in a huge range of shapes and sizes, from simple squares and circles to ornate flowers and flourishes. While not an essential part of card-making they can make for much neater end results and are very handy when producing cards in bulk.

Embossing powders: you can choose coloured embossing powder with a clear ink, or you can choose a coloured ink with clear embossing powder. For best results with fine images, detail is the perfect choice.

Greetings messages: it's worth considering background patterns and a few designs that you can use as main focal images. Messages such as 'Happy Birthday', 'With Love', 'Thinking of You' and similar non gender-based messages will get plenty of use. For background images, a text panel, music and a pattern such as a mesh can be the mainstay of your growing collection. Alphabets are wonderful for spelling out messages and can also be

multi-stamped as backgrounds. For main images the world is your oyster, but be careful what you choose: florals and leaves, for example, are always a safe bet and can be mixed & matched and used continually, each time with a different look.

Inkpads: a potential minefield, so where do you start? If you're going to be stamping in your card-making projects, one of life's absolute essentials is a good black inkpad: one that gives you excellent coverage and is versatile enough for different card surfaces.

Manual die-cutting machine: in order to use dies to cut different materials you will need to purchase a die-cutting machine. The material you want to cut and the die you are using are placed between two cutting plates and fed through the machine. It works like a mangle, putting the plates under pressure in order to cut the die design into your material.

Off-the-shelf embellishments: very handy to have at hand for quick card-making. With so many on the market to choose from, try to pick ones that have a lot of appeal.

Pigment inks: generally, these are what you need if you're going to emboss, as they are slower drying than dye inks and allow you time to emboss.

Punches: hand punches are a cost-effective way of adding decorative main elements, as well as for corner and border decoration.

Rubber stamps: a stamper will probably argue that every rubberstamp in their collection is an essential item, but that's not exactly true! To avoid buying anything that simply looks nice, think about the types of cards that you're planning on making and consider the stamp designs that will be most useful to you.

Card designs

Congratulations

Your step-by-step guide:

1 Crease-fold a piece of 4x5 (½ in) maroon cardstock to form the card base.

2 Ink up a swirl stamp and stamp onto the tea towel fabric.

3 Cut the stamped image out and fray the edges by snipping with the very tip of a pair of scissors.

4 Attach the fabric piece to the front of the card and add a machine-stitched border using light blue thread.

5 Decorate with a paper flower and stud, then add your hand-written greeting and stick.

You will need

- star die
- die-cutting machine
- paper pack
- glitter gems
- blue and brown cardstock
- brown inkpad
- glitter glue

With Love

Your step-by-step guide:

1   Fold the white card in half to form a side-fold base card.

2   Tear a rectangle of white card and pass it through the embossing folder. Matt onto torn pink and then torn purple paper. Secure together with brads in each corner and stick to the front of the card.

3   Tear five petal shapes and a circle for the centre of the flower in contrasting paper. Mount onto the front of the card with 3D foam pads.

4   Embellish with two torn leaf shapes and a tiny tag to write your sentiment.

You will need

- white A5 card
- variety of coloured polka dots
- 4 black brads
- pink paper string
- embossing folder
- green and white scrap card

Celebrate Flower

Your step-by-step guide:

1. Crease-fold an 8x6 in piece of yellow cardstock to form the card base and draw a double black pen border. Fill the inside of the border with white paint and allow to dry.

2. Add black pen dots around the inside of the border and hand-write your greeting.

3. Stamp the arrow five times onto assorted colours of felt and cut out. Fold the stem of each over and secure using a brad layered through a paper flower.

4. Pass a length of ribbon through all the pieces and, starting at one end of the card, secure with a staple between each felt piece.

You will need

- yellow cardstock
- assorted colours of felt
- white acrylic paint
- black pen
- polka dot ribbon
- paper flowers
- pink flower brads
- black inkpad
- stapler
- arrow stamp

Sparkle Flower

Your step-by-step guide:

1 Stamp, colour and cut out the stamp of your choice. Layer a square of paper onto card. Attach to the card with foam pads.

2 Glue the circle to two daisies together and stick to your card.

3 Dot crystals around the paper and on the stamped girl. Mount your image to your card with foam pads to finish.

You will need

- 6x6 in green card
- stamp template of your choice
- green papers
- cardstock
- corner rounder punch
- dye inks
- large daisies
- crystals
- small circle punch

Pretty Daisy

Your step-by-step guide:

1 Trace a petal onto the chipboard and cut out. Use this as a template to cut out six more. Paint them blue and leave to dry.

2 Create a white base card and lightly brush blue paint around the edges.

3 Once the paint is dry, glue the chipboard shapes in place. Outline the petals in black pen and use string to form the stem and flower centre.

You will need

- white textured cardstock
- string
- chipboard
- blue paint
- pencil
- black pen

Cherry Blossom Fan

Your step-by-step guide:

1 Cover the front of an A6 card with dark purple pearlescent cardstock. Stamp a panel of pearlescent lilac cardstock with the cherry blossom branch from the oriental stamp set and attach it.

2 Attach a 2.5 cm strip of the green side of a chosen patterned paper across the width of the card, along with a thin strip of purple striped paper.

3 Cut five pattern repeats (all slots) of the heart design onto the pink side of a different patterned paper. Cut around the edge of the cutting template to produce a shaped edge, then score and fold the cut loops, interlacing them. Cut off the loops at the right-hand end of the design, at the point at which they should be folded.

4 Trim the bottom edges of the interlaced design to create a fan shape. Matt onto purple cardstock and add a gold handle. Lightly emboss a swirl design onto the handle using a scoring tool, then attach the fan to the front of the card.

5 Cut a pink flower from the first chosen patterned paper, add a pink brad to the centre and attach to the card front to finish.

You will need

- hearts template
- 12x12 in glittered patterned papers
- variety of cardstock
- oriental stamp set
- red inkpad
- pink brad

Cherry Blossom Butterflies

Your step-by-step guide:

1. From the pink patterned paper, cut the outer four slots of the entire ring of hearts. This will create just two loops to be folded for each heart. Cut around the outline of the template, then fold and interlace the loops.

2. Attach the interlaced design to pale green pearlescent cardstock and trim. Stick to a square card and trim the card to fit.

3. Cut a branch of glittered cherry blossom from a different patterned paper and attach to the card front.

4. Cut and fold three origami butterflies (two large and one small) from the mulberry paper and attach to the card front to finish.

You will need

- hearts template
- 12x12 in glittered patterned papers
- green pearlescent cardstock
- pink mulberry paper

Pretty Leaf

Your step-by-step guide:

1. Fold 15x30 cm ivory cardstock in half to form a mountain-fold base card.

2. Paint a 13 cm square onto purple paper using a wet paintbrush and tease out. Adhere to the card front.

3. Paint a 9 cm square onto pink paper and tease out.

4. Prick stitch holes onto the pink paper square and draw in faux stitches.

5. Paint a leaf shape onto lime green paper and tease out, fold and pass through a paper corrugator. Open and adhere to your card.

6. Cut a long strip of the yellow paper and tie into a bow. Stick to the front of the card.

You will need

- ivory cardstock
- variety of coloured paper
- dry stick glue
- paper-piercing tool
- silver pen
- paper corrugator
- pink inkpad

21

A Quaint Note

Your step-by-step guide:

1 Cover the card front with patterned paper, distressing the edges with chosen ink.

2 Cut a greeting panel from the patterned paper and attach to the centre of the card.

3 Position the paper flowers down the left-hand side of the panel, making sure the large brown flower is centred over the brown flourish.

4 Add the remaining paper flowers to the bottom right-hand corner of the panel, before embellishing each with an adhesive pearl and brown square button.

You will need

- cream 115 mm blank square card
- brown square buttons
- patterned papers
- coloured paper flowers
- blue and brown adhesive pearls
- inkpad

Oriental Lantern

Your step-by-step guide:

1 Create a 2 ¾ x 7 ¼ in card from red cardstock. Using the oriental templates, cut out a row of three teabag folding papers, leaving narrow borders around them. Fix to the centre of the card.

2 Place a lantern image and two of the symbols from the template sheet onto pearlescent cardstock. Colour in the lantern and the borders with a black gel pen.

3 Trim around each image, leaving a narrow border around the lantern image and fix to each square on the card. The characters should be fixed flat with double-sided tape and the lantern should be raised with 3D foam pads.

You will need

- oriental templates
- red card
- pale yellow pearlescent cardstock
- 3D foam pads
- black gel pen

Cherry on Top

Your step-by-step guide:

1. Print off a cupcake template and cut out the large cupcake topper. Matt with silver mirri card and green card.

2. Line the inside of an aperture card with cupcake backing paper so that it is visible through the aperture. Create a dashed line around the outside of the aperture with a glitter pen.

3. Mount the matted cupcake image over the aperture. Create a slit towards the bottom of the card spine and wrap with a length of red ribbon, tying in a knot at the front.

4. Add gloss medium to the cherry on the cupcake and set aside to dry properly to finish.

You will need

- cupcake template
- silver mirri card
- green cardstock
- white aperture card
- red ribbon
- gloss medium
- green glitter pen
- 3D foam pads

White Dragonflies

Your step-by-step guide:

1 Trim two co-ordinating patterned papers to 11 cm and 9 cm square, layer together and matt with maroon cardstock, leaving a wide border around the edges.

2 Wrap green ribbon around the bottom of the panel and tie into a knot. Attach to the front of a white 13 cm-square card.

3 Punch three dragonflies from dotty paper and attach to the centre of the card using 3D foam pads. Highlight the dragonfly bodies with gems to finish.

You will need

- white card
- maroon cardstock
- patterned papers
- green ribbon
- adhesive gems
- dragonfly punch
- gems

Bouquet

Your step-by-step guide:

1 Cover a square card with gold paper.
   Tear a square of orange
   hand-made paper, ink the edges brown
   and adhere to the centre of the card.

2 Stick a light orange skeleton leaf
   to the centre of the orange
   hand-made square.

3 Create a mini bouquet of flowers by
   cutting three lengths of craft wire,
   bending into shape and gluing pearl
   flower heads to the top of the length.
   Tie a brown ribbon bow at the bottom
   and attach to the leaf.

You will need

- gold paper
- craft pack
- brown inkpad
- orange pearly flowers
- craft wire
- brown ribbon

Fields of Flowers

Your step-by-step guide:

1. Stamp the flower swirl in the centre of a cream card, heat-embossing for definition if you prefer.

2. Cover the front of the card with a 135 mm square of blue cardstock, removing a 50 mm square from its centre to create a frame.

3. Cut a 125 mm square from the reverse of patterned paper and trim diagonally to make four triangles.

4. Lay each triangle onto the card front and fold the centre point of each triangle out to the edge, revealing the blue cardstock and the stamped flower swirl.

5. Decorate the frame with paper flowers and embellish with adhesive pearls to finish.

You will need

- cream 145 mm-square card
- patterned paper
- blue cardstock
- clear stamps
- brown and blue adhesive pearls
- brown, blue and latte paper flowers
- chalk inkpad

Shake a Tail Feather

Your step-by-step guide:

1   Trim orange paper to fit the front of a white card, edge with distress ink and attach.

2   Stamp your image onto white cardstock using a brown inkpad and colour using marker pens. Add gloss medium and die-cut into a scalloped circle. Matt with a slightly larger scalloped circle die-cut from blue paper and attach to the right-hand side of the card.

3   Tie a ribbon bow and attach to the card, along with paper flowers. Using the jewel template, make a flourish on the left-hand side of the card using pearls and gems.

4   Cut a wavy rectangle from orange spotty paper and a sentiment strip from white and blue pearlised cardstock. Edge with your choice of ink, assemble then stamp with your sentiment using another choice of ink to create your insert.

You will need

- white A6 pearlised card
- white cardstock
- marker pens
- brown inkpad
- jewel template
- gloss medium
- brown gingham ribbon

- patterned paper and co-ordinating cardstock
- variety of inkpads
- circle and rectangle dies
- white self-adhesive pearls and blue tear gems
- duck stamp
- cherry paper flowers

Purple Flowers

Your step-by-step guide:

1. Cut purple cardstock to fit the front of a 15 cm square white card, leaving a narrow border around the edges.

2. Stamp the larger corner violet image onto pale lilac cardstock using distress ink and spray with water. Once dry, trim to measure 13.5 × 7.5 cm and stick across the bottom of the card.

3. Trim a piece of white embossed cardstock to fit the top half of the card, attach and use a die-cut purple border to cover the join.

4. Stamp your image onto white cardstock using black ink, colour using marker pens and heat-emboss with embossing powder.

5. Die-cut your image into a circle and mount onto a scalloped circle die-cut from purple cardstock. Mount in the centre of the card to finish.

You will need

- flower stamp set
- white embossed cardstock
- crest cardstock
- circle and scalloped circle dies
- set of marker pens

- foamboard
- black inkpad
- distress ink
- purple and light purple cardstock
- embossing powders

Cutie Pie

You will need

- white and pink cardstock
- white cotton fabric
- patterned paper
- cage stamp
- pink ribbon
- black inkpad
- distress ink
- marker pens
- pinking shears
- brayer
- scalloped edge punch
- glue gel

Your step-by-step guide:

1. Create a white 12.5 cm square base card. Cut a piece of pink cardstock to 12x13 cm, punch a border down the right and stick.

2. Cut a piece of patterned paper to 10x11.5 cm, tie a piece of ribbon around it, tie in a knot then secure to the card front.

3. Stamp the cage image onto white cotton fabric.

4. Using a brayer, colour the fabric with distress inks.

5. Add detail to the image using marker pens and trim using pinking shears. Matt onto fabric. Add a piece of cardstock to the back of the image panel, then attach it to the card front at an angle using glue gel.

Zigzag Patches

Your step-by-step guide:

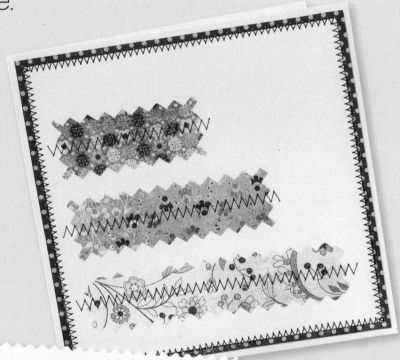

1 Matt a 14 cm square piece of white cardstock onto patterned paper leaving a narrow border.

2 Using zigzag scissors, cut three 2.5 cm wide strips of patterned paper, one 6.5 cm long, one 9 cm long and one 11.5 cm long. Attach to the cardstock panel.

3 Add a zigzag stitch across the three patterned paper strips.

4 Zigzag-stitch around the edges of the white cardstock panel then secure to the card front to finish.

You will need

- white 15.5 cm square card
- white card
- patterned paper
- zigzag scissors
- sewing machine
- sewing thread
- silicone glue

Pink Zinnia

Your step-by-step guide:

1. Stamp a border using embossing enamel onto a pink 15.2 cm-square card. Smudge with brown chalk. Apply vivid chalk colours to pink cardstock large enough for two flowers.

2. Stamp two flowers onto pink cardstock using watermark ink. Dust with embossing enamel and heat. Cut out one full flower and trim away the outer petals of the second. Stamp and emboss a flower centre using embossing enamel and trim.

3. Curl the petals of the smaller flower around a pencil.

4. Wrap a piece of ribbon around the card front, above the stamped border and tie in a knot.

5. Assemble the two flowers and stick to the card front. Add glue to the flower centre and dust with mica fragments. Allow to dry, then attach using 3D foam pads.

You will need

- pink and brown cardstock
- flower stamp
- embossing enamels
- mica fragments
- watermark inkpad
- brown ribbon
- brown, red, orange and purple chalk
- 3D foam pads

House

Your step-by-step guide:

1 Using the window pane shape die with the magnetic window positioned in the top corner, cut your card from yellow colour core cardstock.

2 Use the same die to cut a white piece of card, trim around the window shape to create a frame and glue into position.

3 Take a piece of orange card and use a ruler and pencil to draw a roof shape, using the partly made card as your size guide. Cut out the roof and secure into position with double-sided tape.

4 Matt a purple cardstock rectangle onto white card and add a large brad to resemble a door knob. Fix your door onto the front of the card using foam pads for added dimension.

5 Finish by attaching concertina folded patterned paper to the inside of the card to resemble curtains, adding a thin rectangle of card to the roof section to make a chimney.

You will need

- colour core cardstock
- shape cutting machine
- window pane shaper
- brad
- foam pads

Double Hanging Flower

Your step-by-step guide:

1. Fold a 10x20 cm rectangle of purple cardstock and matt the inside with white paper to create your card.

2. Attach a 5 cm band of patterned paper to the bottom of your card, then add a 1 cm wide strip of yellow card.

3. Open the card flat and turn it over. With a ruler and pencil draw a line 3 cm from each edge, a line 4 cm from the top edge and another line 5 cm from the bottom edge.

4. Use a sharp craft knife and ruler to cut out the rectangle that you have created.

5. Take a 13 cm length of nylon thread and attach to the inside of your card with tape.

6. Die-cut four flower shapes and stick them back-to-back using PVA glue, sandwiching the thread between the layers.

7. Using the scallop square die and green cardstock, create a scalloped shape and trim before attaching to the right-hand side of the card.

You will need

- colour cardstock
- patterned paper
- embossing machine
- flowers die
- scallop square die
- nylon thread
- ribbon

Stroke of Midnight

Your step-by-step guide:

1   Score and fold lilac cardstock in half widthways to make an A5 card. Cut choice of decorative paper to fit the card front, matt with silver mirror card and attach.

2   Cut a strip of silver mirror card and die-cut a swirly pattern in the centre. Attach the negative to the left-hand side of the card.

3   Make a clock face using the template, clock hands dies and peel-off numbers and attach to the left-hand side of the card front with 3D foam. Decorate the inside of the card with decorative paper.

4   Score and fold a 29x21 cm piece of purple card widthways into four equal panels. Cut a circle in the middle of the central panels and decorate the outer two panels with silver mirror card, decorative paper and silver die-cut swirls.

5   Use frosted acetate to make another clock face and attach to the central panels with chain links, to dangle in the aperture.

6   Attach the inner card to the outer A5 card by the two outer panels only. Finish with flat-backed gems.

You will need

- purple and lilac cardstock
- silver mirror card
- die cut swirls
- clock hands template
- decorative paper
- flat-backed gems
- silver brads
- silver chain links

Pink Rose

Your step-by-step guide:

1 Crease-fold a 13.5 cm square piece of white card to create your card base.

2 Cut a piece of lavender card to fit the card front, leaving a narrow border around the edges.

3 Use a scoring tool to score horizontal and vertical lines onto the lavender panel and add small drops lavender pearls at each intersection as shown. Wrap ribbon around the bottom of the panel and fix to the card.

4 Cut small squares of green and white card and layer together.

5 Punch several heart shapes from pink cardstock and paint with pink pearls. Once dry, layer up the heart shapes and push a brad through all the layers, shaping the petals in your hand to form a rose shape.

6 Cut leaves from green cardstock, trim fringing around the edges and stick behind the rose. Mount the finished flower onto the layered squares, then secure to the centre of the card.

You will need

- white, pink, green and lavender cardstock
- pink and lavender pearls
- heart punch
- bone folder/scoring tool
- brad
- paintbrush
- ribbon
- glue

Ribbon Squares

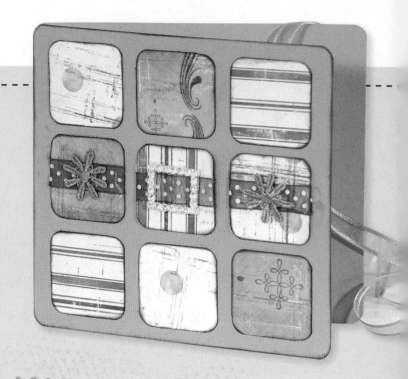

Your step-by-step guide:

1 Crease-fold a 30x15 cm piece of card to create the base card and round the corners.

2 Punch three squares each from three different patterned papers; round all the corners. Ink the edges of each square, as well as the card edges.

3 Stick the squares, evenly spaced, onto the card. Fix pieces of ribbon across each of the central three squares to create the illusion of weaving, adding a diamanté ribbon slide to the middle ribbon before attaching.

4 Cut two flowers from the braid and add over the ribbon to finish.

You will need

- cardstock
- square and corner-rounder punches
- floral braid
- ribbon slide
- polka dot ribbon
- patterned papers
- pink fluid chalk inkpad

Orchid

Your step-by-step guide:

1 Score an A4 sheet of card in half to make an A5 card.

2 Print out your backing paper and trim to 200×137 mm. Edge all four sides with a gold pen and attach to your base card using double-sided tape.

3 Mount your largest topper onto a 155×90 mm piece of gold mirri card using 3D foam tape, then stick to the centre of the card.

4 For extra depth, trim the inner section of another topper and attach over the original using 3D foam tape.

5 Découpage three orchids from an offcut of the backing paper and attach to the bottom right-hand corner of the topper using gel glue.

6 Wrap organza ribbon around the spine of the card and tie into a bow to finish.

You will need

- gentle gloss photo paper
- card
- gold mirri card
- organza ribbon
- double-sided & 3D foam tape
- gold calligraphy pen
- gel glue
- découpage snips

Shaker Card

You will need

- colour core cardstock
- patterned paper
- embossing machine
- card
- window pane die kit
- double-sided tape

- flower magnetic die
- foam pads
- seed beads
- ribbon

Your step-by-step guide:

1. Using the die with the magnetic flower shape positioned in the bottom corner, create your yellow colour core card.

2. Stick a piece of acetate to the inside of the card to cover the aperture you have created. Use a double layer of foam pads to create a wall around the aperture shape on the inside of the card, ensuring there are no spaces between the foam pads.

3. Put small seed beads inside the wall of foam pads and cover with a piece of orange card.

4. Turn the card over and attach a piece of patterned paper to cover half of the front, then decorate with a length of knotted ribbon held with double-sided tape.

Birthday Wishes

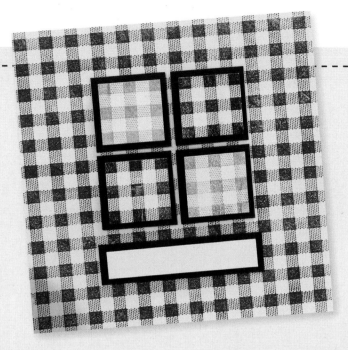

Your step-by-step guide:

1 Stamp the gingham image onto the card front using black ink.

2 Stamp the same image onto white cardstock using purple and blue ink.

3 Cut two purple and two blue 2.5 cm squares from these pieces and stick onto purple cardstock using 3D foam pads. Secure to the card front as shown.

4 Write your birthday words onto white cardstock using black ink and cut out one of the sentiments. Matt onto purple cardstock using 3D foam pads, then stick below the stamped squares to complete your design.

You will need

- gingham stamp
- acrylic block
- white 13.5 cm-square card
- white & purple cardstock
- purple, blue and black inkpads
- sticky tape
- 3D foam pads

Ladybirds

Your step-by-step guide:

1 Sew twice around the edge of the card front using red thread, once using a straight stitch and then with a wide zigzag stitch.

2 Punch two red and two black 1 in circles. Cut the red circles in half and glue on top of the black circles with the top tips overlapping, creating wings. Add three black pearls to each wing.

3 Punch two ½ in black circles and stick under the 1 in black circles where the red tips meet, forming the bugs' heads.

4 Position the green flowers along the base of the card and add a green button to the centre of each one.

5 Place the completed ladybirds onto the card using 3D foam pads and add a sentiment in the top right-hand corner.

You will need

- white card
- black and red cardstock
- light green flowers
- green buttons

- black self-adhesive pearls
- red thread
- black pen
- ½ in and 1 in circle punches
- sewing machine

Toadstool House

Your step-by-step guide:

1. Sew twice around the edge of the card face using a straight stitch in light blue thread.

2. To make the toadstool, punch a red 1 ¾ in circle and trim the base. Stick three white ½ in circles on top. Punch a yellow 1in circle and attach to the card using tape. Place the head of the toadstool above this using 3D foam pads.

3. To make the flower, punch one white and five blue ¾ in circles. Position the blue circles so they overlap one another around the white circle. Decorate the centre of the flower using three yellow self-adhesive pearls.

4. Attach the flower to the card using 3D foam tape and draw a stem in black pen. Cut a green ¾ in circle in half to make two leaves and stick on opposite sides of the stem.

5. Punch small green circles using the ¼ in and 1/16 in punches and attach under the toadstool. Draw tiny stems using a black pen.

6. Write or stamp a sentiment at the top of the card to finish.

You will need

- white card
- red, blue, green, yellow and white cardstock
- yellow self-adhesive pearls
- light blue thread
- black pen
- 1/16 in, ¼ in, ½ in, ¾ in, 1 in and 1 ¾ in circle punches
- sewing machine

Cowboy

Your step-by-step guide:

1 Cut out the horseshoe, riding cowboy and three stars from the template.

2 Trim two rectangular mounts from dark brown cardstock, one approximately 4 cm shorter than the other. Matt and layer a variety of patterned paper from the stack onto the mounts as shown.

3 Spray the riding cowboy with spray gloss to create a glossy effect and fix to the smaller rectangular mount using 3D foam pads. Arrange the panels onto the front of an orange 8 cm square card.

4 To make the cowboy, follow the instructions provided in the pack to assemble.

5 Assemble, then mount onto the right-hand panel of the card before adding peel-offs and facial details to finish.

You will need

- 8 in square card
- cowboy theme template
- pale pink cardstock
- glue
- paper stack
- brown cardstock
- varnish spray gloss
- clear self-adhesive gemstones
- peel-offs
- 3D foam pads

Strips of Scraps

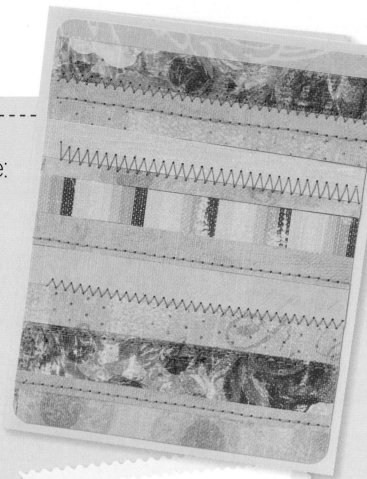

Your step-by-step guide:

1 Crease-fold a 8 ½ x 5 ½ in piece of cream cardstock to create a side-fold card.

2 Cut a 4 x 5 ¼ in panel from scrap paper and cover with 4 in strips of leftover patterned papers. Use strips of varying width and try to keep the colours balanced.

3 Using a sewing machine, stitch across the panel, using a combination of straight and zigzag stitches of different widths.

4 Round the corners and stick to the card front using double-sided tape.

You will need

- cream cardstock
- patterned paper strips
- pink thread
- sewing machine
- corner-rounder punch
- double-sided tape